UNDERSTANDI

YOUR
10 YEAR-OLD

YOUR
10 YEAR-OLD

Jonathan Bradley

Warwick Publishing

Toronto   Los Angeles

ISBN 1-894020-10-3

Published by:
Warwick Publishing Inc., 388 King Street East, Toronto, Ontario M5V 1K2
Warwick Publishing Inc., 1424 N. Highland Avenue, Los Angeles, CA 90027

Distributed by:
Firefly Books Ltd., 3680 Victoria Park Avenue, Willowdale, Ontario M2H 3K1

First published in Great Britain in 1993 by:
Rosendale Press Ltd.
Premier House
10 Greycoat Place
London SW1P 1SB

Design: Diane Farenick

Printed and bound in Canada

CONTENTS

Tavistock Clinic

The Tavistock Clinic, London, was founded in 1920, in order to meet the needs of people whose lives had been disrupted by the First World War. Today, it is still committed to understanding people's needs though, of course, times and people have changed. Now, as well as working with adults and adolescents, the Tavistock Clinic has a large department for children and families. This offers help to parents who are finding the challenging task of bringing up their children daunting and has, therefore, a wide experience of children of all ages. It is firmly committed to early intervention in the inevitable problems that arise as children grow up, and to the view that if difficulties are caught early enough, parents are the best people to help their children with them.

Professional Staff of the Clinic were, therefore, pleased to be able to contribute to this series of books to describe the ordinary development of children, to help in spotting the growing pains and to provide ways that parents might think about their children's growth.

INTRODUCTION

The year between ten and eleven is a time of transition. Though less obviously associated with change than eleven, it is nevertheless a time when your child will be discovering that the rules of life are becoming increasingly complicated. There is a dawning realization that the world is bigger and more uncomfortable than has seemed the case up until now. This can be very overwhelming at times and it might seem that ten year-olds change back and forward, perhaps quite dramatically, from being confident and at ease, to being quite lost, as if in a skin and a personality too large for them. Such lack of confidence and vulnerability can come as quite a shock both to the ten year-old and to you as parent.

The times of vulnerability might seem difficult to understand when put alongside the development of confidence in so many areas. One such area has been in friendships. Children who until now have perhaps needed you to arrange when they see their friends and to organize their time for them are now beginning to be much more independent. The nature of friendships is changing. Friends are likely to be judged now not only by the games they play but also by their perceived qualities of loyalty and steadfastness. When important principles are betrayed, there will be a fierce falling out and the loneliness that follows can be felt very deeply. Similar tensions between a developing social presence and a feeling of isolation can make themselves strongly felt at school. Ten year-olds who with some confidence are finding out where they are placed within the classroom and school setting, can change quickly into the one who is challenging classmates, arguing copiously about matters of justice and becoming overwhelmed by the experience of being rejected.

At home the relationship with you, the parent, is complicated as well. To try out new kinds of friendships, to be concerned in a new and developing way with issues of principle, and be prepared to be faced with the consequences of disappointment and disillusion—all this can be so appealing precisely because it is so unguarded. There can at such times be very strong feelings of wanting to protect your ten year-old from being hurt. But what of other times? Your attempts to be a friend and protector can be rebuffed. This is not necessarily the younger child you knew, for whom the fall from one state to another wasn't so great. Now there can be the added complication of having to deal with the experience of humiliation—of having fallen from a great height. It can be a delicate matter, a foretaste of dealing with an adolescent, not a much younger child. A parent has to tread a delicate line to know how to respect the efforts of their ten year-old to manage the greater challenges of a bigger world than up to this point, to allow falls without clutching back too close.

There are other moments when you might be strangers rather than in a parent-child relationship, when you would love to know what your child is feeling and thinking. Hobbies, often very important at this age, can sometimes seem like a barrier between you. Pursuits such as computer games can be of the solitary kind, and it might seem that part of the reason for them is to shut things out, to provide a place where adults don't belong, or even to provide some inner space to go to which will free them for the moment from having to think about nagging worries and troubles.

The following chapters will look in more detail at some of the complicated issues facing your ten year-old child. It would be a pity however if the book were used as some quick refence, as if your child could be compared against an accurate check list of strengths and weaknesses, or, worse still, in which you will be given detailed lists of do's and don'ts. You will be far better aware than I can be of the very many aspects to your child's personality. But it is possible to be so close that you can't see very well. I hope that gathering themes together might help to give an overall picture, though some parts may be more directly relevant than others to your particular child, in your particular family. Above all, I hope that examples drawn from incidents involving ten year-old children will allow you to see the kind of problems that other ten year-olds and other parents have been confronted with and how they resolved them.

CHAPTER ONE

A DEVELOPING MIND

Top of the mountain

An understandable reaction on reaching ten would be that it marks a landmark rather than a year of transition. Indeed, reaching double figures makes the tenth birthday seem an important one. After all, for a long time ten was where they stopped counting. Actually achieving the figure in real years therefore feels like a milestone reached, and inevitably involves an element of looking back. Many ten year-olds feel that ten is like reaching the top of a mountain from which they seem very big and younger children very small.

When they started school at four or five, children could see what they needed to learn: to swim; to ride a bike; to catch a ball; to skip with a rope; to read; to write; and, though this one is hazier, to handle numbers. All these things by ten, by and large, children can not only do, but do well.

Physical skills

It might seem to ten year-olds that they can master most things to do with their body. Many games and sports involve running, but they can master complicated steps such as hopscotch, and dodge the ball easily. Out of interest in what their bodies can do they can set themselves prodigious endurance tests and readily become involved in sponsored events which pose such a challenge. Intricate co-ordination skills are developed in games such as soccer or racquet sports and hours can be spent, when alone, throwing balls against walls and practicing kicking or catching. Challenges such as climbing up trees or other obstacles, or water sports are all a serious way of life for many ten year-olds. The need to exercise and the pleasure of it are, it seems, given added impetus by the absence of noticeable internal physiological changes. In particular, menstruation for girls is usually some time away at the beginning of the tenth year and while the body's shape is gradually changing it is the refined muscle tone and posture which is more readily noticed. Boys too are some years away from the genital changes associated with the beginnings of adolescence.

The confidence in the strength and additional reliability of the ten year-old's body, which leads to the setting of targets of strength and endurance and co-ordination, forms a natural base from which to explore and develop friendships. At the beginning of the year such friendships or pairings are often based on doing things together rather than on any exploring of the meaning and quality of friendship in a reflective sense.

All in the mind

There is a mental change too that occurs at this time. Having spent the last five years learning the rules of how to do things and practicing applying them, children during this year may begin to look for wider patterns behind the rules, to try to figure things out for themselves. An example will help to make the point clear. When a number of children of different ages were asked to play a game which was like "Twenty Questions" they approached it in very different ways. In the game the children were asked to find a word on a page by asking as few questions as possible. Younger children had no trouble at all with how to play. They picked out one word straightaway and were very puzzled when it wasn't the right one. Guess followed inspired guess, with not much sign of an overall plan. But at ten, the children were usually more able to sit back and think about the problem. After a few guesses they begin to realize that if you ask about bigger parts of the page it doesn't matter whether the answer is "Yes" or "No" because both answers help in the search.

Strategies

The way that ten year-olds can now try to work out this problem gives some clue to the changes that are taking place at this time. When faced with a puzzle that they can't solve, ten year-olds can be very sure at first that the answer will be given to them by some sort of inspired guess. But when their guesses don't work then it is possible for them to take a wider approach to the problem. Older children of eleven or twelve upwards will on the whole try a strategy from the beginning.

It is only a game and one which seems at first sight to require little preparation or thought. In fact this isn't the case. In order to play well it is important to plan and to realize that overall, it is far better to give up solving the puzzle very quickly by lucky guesses which are very unlikely to be right, and to try instead to work out a plan, which can then be used for lots of "finding" games. Ten year-olds playing this game are learning how to work out plans which will help them to meet new situations, confident that they have the strength to deal with them. This is very hard to do, and when asked how they felt about having learned a new way of playing "Twenty Questions" it was clear that the ten year-olds were of two minds. They were clearly pleased that they had worked out a method of solving the problem and wanted to keep on trying it to see if it really worked. It was also clear that they felt that somehow the game wasn't as exciting as it had been. It is quite understandable that having a plan which can work if it is followed would also reduce the thrill of a chance of a lucky guess. But there was more to it than this. When asked about the game many of the ten year-olds were not just disappointed that the thrill had gone out of it. They were also surprised that the way of solving the puzzle by guessing hadn't worked. One boy when asked if he could explain why he had guessed a particular word, explained that "a voice inside his head" told him what the answer was. It was as if he felt that the "voice" really did know what the answer was. It was a shock at first that the voice had let him down. It was as if an "inside friend" who could be trusted to give the right answer had all of a sudden been shown to be not as able as had been thought.

"Old" methods versus "new" methods

Although the above examples are concerned with how ten year-olds are developing greater mental abilities, there are similarities between what ten year-olds are having to face in this area and what they are facing in those of emotional development and social relations. It can be a shock to come across problems to which the answer seemed obvious, and realize that it isn't as clear as was first thought. It can be very tempting to hold on to old methods, to try to make them work, or to come back to them as an escape from the strain of trying to understand more complicated rules. On the other hand it is possible to treat the old approaches as babyish and move away altogether from familiar ways of looking at things, as if they can't still continue to be relevant. Other chapters will be looking at different areas of development. Common to all, particularly as ten year-olds move towards their eleventh birthday, are the mixed feelings resulting from learning some thing more complicated but having as a result to leave behind something that is more comforting and familiar.

CHAPTER TWO

SCHOOL LIFE

Having to cope with differences

School will be for many children the place where they will be becoming increasingly aware of where they stand in relation to others and increasingly puzzled by areas of incompetence, as well as of achievement, within themselves. The most glaring difference perhaps, brought more sharply into focus by the growing use of standardized tests, will be differences in academic achievement. Children will be quick to notice what sets or groups other children are in, and almost invariably will be ranking themselves against their classmates (or ranking others in terms of their own abilities). Quite regardless of what the school policy may be, children of this age tend to know exactly where they (and everyone else!) come in the pecking order They will also be noticing social and cultural differences. The ten year-old will be becoming aware for example that friends and children in the class are quite differently placed in terms of where they live and what the level of the family's wealth is. Stories from countries which are much poorer, particularly if they happen to be a country of cultural origin for some of the children, will impinge very deeply. How to cope with differences is quite a problem.

Two different ways of hiding distress

Here are two examples of children who were troubled by their performance in school and tried to cope with it in their own way.

Susan

Susan, the oldest of three girls in her family, was usually thought of as a very amenable cheery girl, very popular at school and appreciated by the teachers. She was confident in all areas of her schoolwork except in reading, where she was comparatively slow although not behind the class in general. Reading had become a specific block to her and despite sympathetic attention by teachers, she had begun to anticipate judgment and failure where there was none. Over time the stress that she felt in relation to reading seemed to spill over into other areas of her life, even those areas where she had felt confident until then. Eventually things came to a head on Field Day. Parents were invited, and as Susan was quite athletic she was expected to do well. However, within a short distance of the start of her race, Susan broke down, sobbing and screaming for her mother. She had to be helped back to the start, clinging to her mother like a much smaller child. To everyone's surprise it turned out that Susan was not physically hurt, it was just that she suddenly felt that she couldn't go on.

Through this drama, which was taken seriously both by her mother and by the school, Susan drew attention to her distressed state of mind. They, as well as she, then realized that her difficulty with reading was not an isolated thing which could be ignored, but had a deeper effect, threatening to undermine her confidence generally, leaving her feeling quite literally "unfit to compete."

This kind of breakdown can lead to a useful breakthrough in development. The stage was now set for Susan to bring her own inner resources to bear on the problem which had previously been an inaccessible block, to make use of the help made available to her by her teacher.

Alan

Alan reacted in quite a different way. He was a child with general learning difficulties and came from a home where discipline was on the strict side. Alan had difficulty adapting to the other children in the family. His external appearance however gave no hint of weakness. He was fascinated, in his play, by military tactics. At home he was becoming obsessed by videos portraying aggression, and the stories he wrote and pictures he drew at school were about war and the kind of scars that can be inflicted in a war. It might be thought that his preoccupation with violence might show itself in bullying and aggression at school and at home. But in fact he was normally a timid child, the victim of quite a bit of teasing and bullying himself. When provoked unduly however, he would transform himself into a merciless attacker, like the video "heroes." Indeed, on one occasion he even arrived in school carrying a baseball bat studded with nails. It was difficult for the school to know what to do, since his attacks, when they came, seemed out of proportion to the provocation. It was necessary to bear in mind that the explosion, although it appeared indiscriminate, was meant to settle countless earlier scores that Alan hadn't been able to deal with at the time, and which had festered, growing in his mind. Looked at from this perspective, he must have felt vulnerable indeed judging by the force needed to face his opponents. For Alan this was clearly no ordinary mayhem of school life, but such a rough battlefield that, in order to survive he had to fill his mind with examples of those who really knew how to deal with enemies, model himself on them, and even climb into their clothes.

Coping with ability

The two previous examples concerned children who have learning difficulties and perhaps as a consequence of this, find that other areas of their life become difficult to cope with. But the pressures might be just as intense for children who are considered to be able. How are they to deal with the experience of being successful and quick academically? There are different possibilities of course. One thing that can happen, which might be thought of as opposite to that described earlier (where learning difficulties seemed to lead to a generalized feeling of vulnerability), is for skill and academic ease to lead to a false sense of security.

Collecting facts or using your mind

Michael was a boy for whom this seemed to have happened. He had become contemptuous in his approach to life, particularly to adults. It seemed when you were talking to him that stupidity was always in the air, whatever the topic. Everything seemed to be treated like an exercise and he seemed to feel an almost compulsive need to name the answer as quickly as possible. There was a brittle, panicky quality to this, as if even the possibility that he might not know the answer could topple him from some precarious pedestal of being "the gifted one." The problem with this approach was that it made it impossible for him to consider broader questions which don't have an obvious answer but need a different approach, that of thinking things through. The way Michael clung to this pedestal—which could be called "knowledgeability"—got in the way of his developing his own thinking powers, his imagination and his mind.

The clown

Other children who are gifted might find the struggle to live up to what is expected too much for them, and abdicate the position. The class clown is a position that can be sought either from the perspective of the non-coping one or the one who finds the strain of being successful too much. The pain of being the one who is laughed at, and who isn't taken seriously, can be a price paid willingly for the short-lived gain that comes from having opted out of the competition.

Stereotypes

The age of ten is where differences and inequalities are being noticed and observed. This is not done just out of interest. The way in which an individual is considered can be decided by quite a small aspect of who they are and what they do. Stereotyping takes place, intentionally or otherwise, and it is interesting to think why. Perhaps, in the world of ten year-olds where differences and inequalities are being thought about a great deal, they tend to stand out as the most important qualities, some of which are wanted, others not. It is understandable that those that aren't wanted should get thought of as belonging to one individual or group. For example, if stupidity is felt to belong to a few people only, it then becomes easier to feel that "stupidity" whatever it is, doesn't belong to oneself. Being subject to such pressure from the group can have a big effect on individual children.

Taking the pressure off

Is there anything that can be done to help children manage the pressure to succeed without losing their confidence on the one hand, or assuming too great confidence, based on arrogance, on the other? Many children seek out a middle position which doesn't reflect their true ability, avoiding being very bad but not being able to be very good, so that they won't stand out. It would be a mistake to try to reduce the anxiety by belittling it or by trying to coax your child to be less anxious. The problem is that from the perspective of a ten year-old it can seem to be an enormity to be falling behind the others. But ten year-olds can be helped to regain perspective on the matter if they can be sure that your affection is not dependent on how well they do. The thought that the failure reflects on you as parent would be a paralyzing one for most children even though they may try to brazen the matter out and pretend that they don't care.

CHAPTER THREE

EMERGING FROM THE CROWD

The stifling of individuality

A teacher was finding it very difficult to cope with her class of ten year-olds. She was a fairly newly qualified teacher, but she had taught ten year-olds before and therefore found it difficult to know why she found it so hard to communicate with this particular class. She was used to motivating the children with her enthusiasm, rather than with control. Her experience with other classes had been that projects were seized on eagerly if somewhat boisterously. Now it was as if her plans met a resistance that came close to truculence. At the beginning of the day, when she would have expected natural exuberance in the class, there was a strangely muted reaction to her suggestions, even from children who did not behave in this way when on their own or in small groups. Other children kept their heads down, obviously ill at ease.

Recently she had started to behave uncharacteristically, by bribing the class to settle down to her plan of the day and by offering them promising rewards later on if they would do what she wanted. As a result she had been achieving less with this class than she felt she ought to. She was worried about this and, unusually for her, had started to become defensive in front of other colleagues about what went on in the classroom.

Within a relatively short space of time her teaching life had become a misery and her health was beginning to pay the price for attempting to go on coping. What troubled her very much, however, was the thought that the children were suffering also. Although what hit her was the defiance of the group as a whole, she knew enough about individual children to realize that many of them were unhappy with what was happening. Mysterious "illnesses" started to occur and the attendance of the class had started to become erratic.

While the above example isn't necessarily typical of what happens in classrooms, it would be interesting to remain with it for a while; it does describe well how powerful a grouping, or more precisely a "ganging up," of ten year-olds can be, and also how being part of such a structure can have quite a high price attached to it in terms of illness, unhappiness and unnatural curbing of enthusiasm. When the classroom experience was explored a little further, some interesting facts emerged.

In the first place it became clear that the actual membership of the class had been remarkably consistent over the past five years. Obviously some children had moved in and out of the group during that time but, overall, a powerful core had moved up together. This was in contrast to the provision of teachers: there had been at least twenty-three separate teachers over the past five years and no less than seven in the previous year! Gradually this had become known to be a "'difficult'" class, one which you had to get on your side if you were to get the best out of them.

A detailed study was carried out of movement and activity within the class. It seemed that the class had made use of the "open plan" layout to create a linking between desks and individuals that was anything but free. There was a powerful grouping of three boys. They occupied desks near the front of the classroom. Interestingly, they didn't always take the lead when negotiating with the teacher what the day's activity would be, and this made it difficult to see what a crucial role they played in maintaining the gang structure. On their journeys across the classroom many children, particularly girls, would go past the three desks even if it was out of their way. Usually they smiled as they went past, sometimes paused for a while and some children even made an act of obeisance such as a nod of the head as they passed.

This class had a hidden, unofficial leadership which must have provided some sense of stability when there had been so many changes of teacher. Of course this support structure, one which attempted to do away with the need for adults, had its drawbacks. It had to occupy more and more of the class activity. As a result, academic performance of the group as a whole suffered.

Once it had been possible to acknowledge with the group what a difficult school life they had, it was also possible for the gang of three to become less vigilant on the class's behalf. As they began to lose their hold, individual children also began to emerge from the group. For some, the emergence had to do with letting it be known they had individual learning difficulties that could be given attention, appropriately by an adult. It was astonishing, however, to see the emergence of individual talent. Without any explicit instructions being given, art became very important within this class. One particularly striking picture that emerged from a hitherto silent and self-effacing girl was of a brilliant sun peeping out from the left hand corner of a dark background. Appropriately, she entitled it "Dawn"!

I have chosen an example of the kind of event that doesn't by any means happen every day because it highlights the pressures which can come from being part of a large group. It can be very difficult to allow one's own voice to be heard in such a circumstance.

The tyranny of clothes

In less dramatic circumstances than those described, fitting in is an important part of everyday life to many ten year-olds. It may be important to find a secure and accepted position in the eyes of one's peer group before daring to establish views and opinions which set one apart from the crowd. One tyranny that confronts most parents is that of fashion. or the need to conform to a particular definition of fashion.

Michael was someone who fitted easily into his peer group. He was a wiry, compact, well co-ordinated boy, perhaps giving the impression of caring less about criticism than he really did. He was certainly very particular about what kind of clothes he should wear. Sneakers had to be of a special kind, bearing his favorite brand name, something which made them more important than their intrinsic qualities such as the type of the sole, etc. It was the outside appearance that mattered most and it had to conform absolutely to the style that was acceptable to children of his own age.

Michael's mother was shopping without him when she spotted a track suit that was good quality, good value and looked good. The problem was that it wasn't the right brand. Michael simply refused to wear it; it wasn't right, it didn't fit in at all with the kind of garment he had in mind. In many areas of life Michael was able to compromise, and his not being able to do so on this occasion suggested that having the right clothes wasn't simply a matter of choosing the fashion of the moment out of a simple choice. The incident gave rise to many more heartfelt feelings than this.

One issue seemed to be about a developing independence: Michael felt he was old enough at ten to decide what he wore. Clearly this move to independence where clothes are concerned doesn't begin with the age of ten and it certainly doesn't end with ten! There is another element about the choice which, paradoxically, isn't at all about freedom of choice. The move to have greater independence from parents was also, for Michael, a move towards greater conformity with the demands set for him by his peer group. It seemed that the greatest anxiety here was not so much about wanting to fit in as a positive choice, but the fear that if he wore the wrong gear he would be rejected. Clearly it is this fear that manufacturers and advertisers of clothes are in tune with. It must be very frustrating to have in the house many separate sets of sports gear that are in perfectly good condition, but are not acceptable any more because the adult team on which the outfit is modeled have changed a tiny detail since you went to the stores. It can be difficult to know what to do in such a situation. Following the latest fashion can be a real drain economically, and trying to buy the latest item rather than strike a compromise will quickly mean that the tyranny of having to fit in which faces your child gets transferred to you as parent in the form of bills which have to be paid. On the other hand, it is not easy to ignore your child's demands to fit in when you can see that a lot depends on staying in with the group.

In Michael's case his mother recognized the importance of the issue and was able to write off the cost of the track suit as a loss. However, it does seem important to recognize the underlying anxieties. Somewhere there seems to be a fundamental polarity which could be expressed at one end as your child thinking, "If I look right they won't 'see' me and so I won't be taunted by them as different," and at the other, "If I wear their uniform they'll let me join and then I can show them what I can do." There is a huge difference between feeling on the one hand that to stick on the appropriate colors will confer membership of the group, and on the other to be sufficiently confident in your own talents to feel that you can share them with the group. In the one case clothes are being seen as a skin giving appropriate camouflage, but in the other they are seen simply as the right clothes for the occasion. There will be many possible positions between these two extremes and, depending on what other pressures are present at the time, the same child will be at differing points on this scale. However, it would be worrisome if at this age children constantly sought to be anonymous within a group, restricted to copying what the others do, rather than being themselves.

Successful teamwork

Undoubtedly one of the joys that can come with being ten is to be part of a successful team. Anthony was overjoyed to be named to the school soccer team. Occasional games were arranged with a local school, close enough geographically to be seen as a rival. Gradually, before the match, Anthony became more and more interested in deciding which professional soccer team to support. Up until this point he had been a collector of cards giving details of individuals, but now the focus of Anthony's collecting became much more sophisticated. Rather than wanting simply to amass a large collection, and letting this be known to his friends, he became much more interested in specializing in those individual players with whom he could identify. Anthony himself had been asked to play in a midfield (or middle of team) position. His coach described it as being a very important one because, given that the soccer pitch was long, only children who were fit enough to run on behalf of the team would be able to link the defenders behind the midfield with the attackers at the front.

Whether or not this presented a sophisticated view of midfield players in soccer, the idea that he might be a "link man" was a tremendously important one for Anthony. The new idea didn't even confine itself to soccer. Once it had taken root in one area (achieved by passionate discussions about the midfield role and focusing on specialist soccer videos) the idea of "linking" as an activity came to be focused on. Having grasped the idea of a link, Anthony became interested in other abstract concepts too. As for the game in question, Anthony's father was amazed at how mature an understanding of the role had been grasped by Anthony who, within a brief period of time, seemed to have made a significant leap forward, not only in soccer skills but in emotional maturity.

As is often the case, the incident had a cautionary ending. After the game, the relief at doing well and contributing undoubtedly to a fine win, as well as the many congratulations he had received from teammates and delighted teachers, were very gratifying. Anthony began to feel that his performance had been that of an international star in the making. Anthony's father became worried that he was talking as if his career decision (to become a soccer player) had already been made. In order to speak to this state of mind Anthony's father intended to say something like, "Let's wait and see what the future holds." What he actually said was, "Soccer is a very hard job and it might be too hard for you." The effect on Anthony was as dramatic as if a soccer ball had burst. The words dashed his hopes.

They were able to talk about the incident later. Anthony's father said that he had become concerned that Anthony was pinning all his hopes for the future on this one success. He himself had been impressed by the other gains that had been made, in terms of academic linking, and nurtured other hopes for Anthony. Anthony's sheer explosion of joy had been too big for him to contain. Rather than see it as the exciting dream of a ten year-old, Father began to think that Anthony had already moved towards serious career decisions.

This chapter has looked at some of the ways in which ten year-olds are very aware of peer-group expectations. The examples have shown what pressure there can be not to stand out from the crowd, even at the risk of losing one's individuality. However, operating within a team can release individual capacities and new insights (as in the case of Anthony). The next chapter focuses more on some of these individual insights, particularly with respect to ten year-olds' growing capacity for friendship.

CHAPTER FOUR

FRIENDSHIP

Friendships are formed long before the age of ten, but nevertheless at about this time changes in the nature of these friendships start to occur. Much will depend on individual circumstances, some of which have been described in previous chapters. Bearing in mind that friendships can be answering differing needs, this chapter will look at some of the issues that are being explored at this time.

Moving outwards

Friendship provides an important opportunity to move away, both emotionally and actively, from a focus within the family, a life dominated by bonds with parents and brothers or sisters. There are already the beginnings of a difficult decision as to whether life is best lived with the help of companions or in solitude. Sometimes it can be difficult to let go of the grip on home in order to explore friendships. For example, Erin and her mother had some very difficult issues to cope with. In particular, Erin missed her father very badly. He had lived with the family until she was six. The break up when he had moved out had been very difficult and only intermittent contact had been kept with him. Unfortunately he would make promises for Erin's birthday which he either did not keep, or else kept in such a way that by the time he finally arrived with the present, Erin would have given up hope. Faced with Erin in such a state of anxiety and floods of tears, Yvonne, her mother, felt it would be better for them both to forget him, and tried to stop him coming to the house.

Over the years this only child and her mother had become very close, drawn closer by the hard time they had shared. Erin had found it difficult to sleep on her own and had become used to waking up in the night and going to Mother's bedroom to spend the rest of the night there. Erin's mother had not minded this, particularly as she herself was recovering from a disastrous relationship. It was also comforting for her to be with Erin rather than on her own.

However, recently Yvonne had started another relationship which seemed like it might be serious. Erin was seething and very unwelcoming. Although she had been very angry with her father she now began to compare him favorably with this newcomer, who was pushing his way into their lives. She seemed to sense that she was about to become the unwanted bed companion and clung to her place with a ferocity that startled Yvonne and led her to feel guilty for not having been stronger. She hadn't realized that Erin had taken to the close relationship with her as if it could close the door on unreliable fathers and promise a life based on security rather than having to manage the tremendous anxiety she was suffering by never knowing if she would be let down.

As Mother's relationship with her friend became more serious, Erin started to wet her bed and also to soil herself during the day. These were problems which had occurred at the time of the original parting between Mother and Erin's father many years before, and had not been as embarrassing then as now, at ten. The next thing was that Erin started to feel sick when it was time to go to school in the morning. At first Yvonne doubted the symptoms were genuine, but as she tried to push Erin into school Erin fainted and several times she vomited in the classroom.

The school realized that Erin needed professional help, but by this time it seemed that the close bond which had enabled Yvonne and Erin to cope with previous difficulties had disappeared. Indeed Yvonne felt rage. She felt that she was being blackmailed into giving up her new relationship. Erin was uncompromising and seemed to be saying, "It's either me or him."

What could have developed into a tragic situation was in fact relieved by Erin herself. She found a friend, Lucy. It seemed to be a bond based on activities such as the Girl Scouts but it developed from there. It took Erin outdoors and away from a relationship with Mother that had become too close to be easily thought about. At first Mother felt keenly the change from being very close to Erin, albeit in a fighting and colliding way. The sudden lack of conflict was something tangible, which left a hole in her life. She began to worry about Erin spending more time out of the house and felt abandoned.

It's hard to say whether Erin was in fact rejecting her mother in the way she turned to her friend Lucy. This friendship didn't seem to have the exclusive qualities of the bond with Yvonne but seemed instead to be based on an exuberant activity. It was as if Erin could only discover how "full of running" she was through the help of her friend Lucy. Lucy showed her a side of herself that she wasn't able to see while locked in battle over Yvonne's relationship with her new partner. There seemed to be little place in her life for bedwetting any more which quickly disappeared, though the difficulties about going to school took longer to resolve, and were helped by attendance at a small learning group for part of the week.

The testing of loyalties

Erin's friendship with Lucy gave her a chance to break free from a situation which was threatening to destroy the home. Her new friendship was, understandably, a chance not to think but to enjoy some good company. In less trying circumstances than these, friendship, while providing companion ship, also makes it possible to examine the rules of friendship. Within such friendships, the fact that loyalties are tested, sometimes to the breaking point, but more usually to the point of a temporary falling out is very important. Undoubtedly feelings run high and this can be trying for parents, as well as being emotionally demanding for children. Often, however, important concepts are being put to the test. Particularly when children have been involved in families where a break-up has taken place, it can be an enormous relief to find themselves in a situation where they are more in control and able to make a relationship endure.

Playing with feelings

Some children, unfortunately, aren't able to maintain individual friendships and instead seek to involve more than one person in the way that they test loyalties, perhaps in the hope that they won't have to face up to issues personally. Linda, for example, was an expert in setting people up for disappointment. She spent quite a lot of time cultivating friendships with girls of her own age and then just at the point when a girl would begin to think that she had found a new friend, Linda would sweetly tell her that she had decided she didn't want to hang around with her and wouldn't be her friend for that day after all. It was as if Linda had made a study of spitefulness and knew from somewhere inside herself that you hurt people more by rejecting them once they have begun to open themselves up to you. She was an expert at having a little coterie whom she used to treat in this way, by some rotation known only to herself. She seemed to know who to choose, particularly girls who liked being chosen by her because she could indeed be a very good friend at first.

This kind of exploitation of friendships certainly can exist among ten year-olds, and it can be a delicate matter knowing when to intervene on behalf of your child. In Linda's case it seemed that there was a reverse side of the coin. She had felt quite secure in her family until the unexpected arrival (from her point of view) of a baby brother ten years younger than her. One way of making sense of the succession of girlfriends that she delighted in paying attention to, only to drop subsequently, was as some complicated way of enacting a drama, with the help of unsuspecting victims, around this unexpected birth of a brother. Not only did they represent what she would have liked to do to her brother, but they provided her with a way of making these other girls have the hurt which she herself couldn't bear to have.

Doubtful friendships

The example of Linda leads to the question of doubtful friendships, and the difficulty this poses for you as parent. The process of friends mutually choosing one another is a complicated one you will have had a lot of exposure to as your child has grown up. Usually, if a friendship doesn't work out, there will be a breaking off and perhaps a joining up again, or a moving over to another friend—children normally know when they are being trapped in a situation that is uncomfortable for them. Part of the experience of making friends is to become better at not being placed in a particular role for a long time, and to negotiate with your friend. But the example of Linda shows that sometimes the gains that children make from a particular friendship can blind them to other things which are taking place, and which in the long run, aren't good. Undoubtedly, some likings or friendships can be based on a fundamental inequality, when one child is meant to fulfill the needs of another, needs which are pursued in quite a compulsive way. I have speculated earlier that part of the way that Linda used her friends was to enact over and over again the feeling of rejection that she experienced with the arrival of her brother. She wanted someone else to bear the rejection. The scene had to be repeated over and over again because she herself didn't have the solution to it. She couldn't heal herself. Her situation was played over with a group. However it can be particularly difficult for you as parent to realize that your child is either being used in a relationship, or is using someone else.

Being dominated

Sara was very friendly with Rachel. What Rachel did, Sara had to do. It was almost as if she was Rachel's shadow following two steps behind, never quite catching up to her. Sara was by nature a dependent child and could easily get herself locked into situations where somebody else made the decisions for her. Sara's parents were worried about this lack of initiative but weren't unduly concerned about Rachel's influence over her. However, Rachel unexpectedly had to go away with her parents for a long break. At first the effect on Sara was devastating. She found it very difficult not sitting beside Rachel at school, not having her to play with, and seemed at a loss to know what to do with herself. And then she gradually became more alive than she had been. She became animated in a way her parents hadn't seen for some time, went back to friendships that she had neglected for quite a while, and seemed to become more vivacious during Rachel's absence which lasted some months. Rachel came back, very quickly sought Sara out and started to dominate her again. Although Sara had seemed to come alive and had seemed to form other friendships, it was as if she couldn't carry inside her a strong enough sense of who she had been without Rachel to prevent herself from being sucked into Rachel's influence again, and being bossed by her.

Bad liaisons

Some relationships seem not merely doubtful but bad for the children concerned and those with whom they come into contact. Undoubtedly there can be bad twinnings and groupings where it seems as if the destructive impulses of one child are aided and abetted by another. Just as children can be creative in each other's company, they can also be destructive, sometimes in perversely inventive ways.

One of the difficulties in accepting that bad relationships can flourish among young children is that we can lose touch with our own childhood and the times when we were vicious. But current events will leave us in no doubt that ten year-old children are very capable of behaving in a violent and sadistic way, even to the point of killing younger children.

Many ten year-olds will be prepared to bully younger children when given the opportunity, though this can be for many complex reasons. For some, other children, particularly younger children, will revive bitter and unwanted memories of their own childhood. There may be other situations when the birth of a baby brother or sister can lead to feelings of rejection. The earlier example of Linda showed how the feelings of being rejected at the time by the birth of her brother were not held inside her, but put onto a succession of willing victims who were meant to feel like the rejected ones instead of herself. Strangely, the urge to find "victims" in this way can be particularly strong if children are making a big effort to overcome feelings of rejection and jealousy. Face to face with an actual baby brother, a child such as Linda might feel deeply protective and loving. At such a time there will be little space for more vicious feelings towards her baby brother.

But if there is a place to be different (and often it is school that provides such an opportunity) then it can be a relief at first to be loving in one place and cruel somewhere else. The relief is often short lived and many children will become deeply anxious if their life gradually seems to be dividing into good and bad places in this way.

Richard was convinced that he knew the answer to his extremely violent rages. He remembered little about what he did during his rages, usually summoned up to defend the reputation of his mother who was known to be a prostitute by children in his class. He felt that the solution was simple however. If only he could go into the hospital then someone could remove the "bit of his brain that did the bad things." In fact he was so convinced that this was the solution that neurological tests were eventually carried out. These did not reveal anything unusual. His words do underlie, however, how frightening it can seem to have lost control of a part of one's brain, and not to know what will happen as a result.

The title of this rather sober part of the chapter is "Bad Liaisons." It might seem strange that it is included within a description of friendship, but in fact the joining together of children who have a bad agenda in mind can take on many of the qualities of friendship, but a friendship in reverse.

43

CHAPTER FIVE

HOBBIES AND PURSUITS

Private space

In the introduction to this book, it was mentioned that hobbies and pursuits of various kinds can come to be a barrier between you and your child. Undoubtedly, there is a very different side to this. Hobbies and pursuits are a very important source of nourishment for ten year-old children; they allow them the space to make gains not only in the particular hobby they are pursuing, but emotional gains which can be hard to make without privacy. In this section I will look at the issue of hobbies and pursuits, both as a rich source of growth and as a possible barrier to communication, both between you and your child and within children themselves.

The bookworm

Reading can be a real pleasure at this age. The skill of reading can be taken for granted, so that children can allow themselves to be carried away into the world of the book. By now they will have had enough experience of reading to be able to seek out the kind of books that will develop their particular fantasies or interests.

At this point the worry may arise for parents that their child is reading something unsuitable. For example, the latest novel by a favorite author was being passed from girl to girl to be read in Barbara's class at school. Barbara, who always had her nose in a book, seemed to be devouring it avidly.

When her mom picked it up and glanced at it though, she looked again. Was this really the same author? Where the other books had been clearly appropriate for this age group, this latest book was highly doubtful, to say the least. The characters were in their later teens, and the relationships the book described were definitely sexual. When this was raised with Barbara, she said, "Oh Mom, it's fine! Everyone else has read it and *their* moms think it's all right."

Barbara's mom was in a quandary about what to do: Was she really making too much of it? Should she lay down the law about what her daughter was allowed to read? Or should she instead be grateful that she was reading at all? She puzzled over this, and in the end what she did was to make an opportunity for Barbara to talk to her about the book, and about things in it she might not understand. In this way it became a useful opening point for an important conversation.

Animals and pets

Younger children of course like animals but, understandably, the care of an animal carried out by a younger child needs to be shared quite a lot with parents and other members of the family. At ten, however, there is a real possibility that children can manage the responsibility themselves. Children do often have difficulty in coming to terms with all of their feelings—that is, keeping both their loving and hating feelings together about their brothers and sisters; we can see how animals provide an opportunity under the one roof for reflecting on care. For some children, having a pet, particularly if it's a small pet, will be a unique opportunity of having a living creature within their control. They are being faced for the first time with the real possibility both of looking after their pet, and also of neglecting it through forgetfulness, that is, unthinking cruelty.

If it is true that, as a recent survey suggested, a lot of adult owners of pets regard them as having the intelligence of an average nine year-old, then it is also true that for many children a pet can provide a way of communicating emotionally to an animal where it is not always easy to speak directly about feelings to parents or to other adults. For example, Jacqueline had a fascination for horses. Not only did she learn to ride but a lot of her spare time would be spent in trying to draw horses. She was critical of her own efforts, though in fact she was quite skilled. But Jacqueline felt that she never succeeded in getting the proportions of the horse right, particularly its sense of power. She was able to describe what a wonderful thing it was to be able to feel safe with a horse. She could pet it, but she also felt that it was immensely strong and could be relied on. She had also begun to practice jumping.

It was difficult for anyone to start a conversation with Jacqueline that wasn't about horses. Certainly she found it difficult to talk about her father and her early years, but little by little did so. She had never known him, since he had died when she was very young. Her mother had to put Jacqueline in foster care after some years and since then she had lived with a succession of relatives. She had received much kindness from them and seemed, at least on the surface, to have settled in well at home and at school. Her early experiences had made her wary of trusting, with the one exception of horses.

There was an interesting connection between Jacqueline's drawings of horses and her visits to the stables where she rode. On her return home she would try to put down on paper her impressions of the horse (whose name she kept to herself). The first drawings after a visit would be bold, well proportioned, have musculature. But then over the days as she drew them again and again they would become smaller, without obvious definition, resembling a dog rather than a horse. This would be so frustrating for Jacqueline who could see her memory of the strong, dependable horse gradually slipping from her mind until it became a caricature. It was impressive, however, to see her persevering, trying to revive the memory of something strong and dependable.

The love of pets and other animals obviously can be used to withdraw from relationships, but animals can also help to repair damaged feelings, in a gentle way.

Computer and video games

It is difficult to generalize about computer or video games because they can be used to fulfill so many different functions. They certainly seem to fit in very well with the ten year-old's natural aptitude and quickness of response. A clear distinction should be made between games which are felt to supply a missing need, and those which are for enjoyment's sake. From the point of view of parents, it is important to distinguish between those games and playing time which provide a welcome diversion, and games which are used to create an exclusion zone—"adults keep out!" David, for example, was a solitary boy, one who used to find it difficult to establish friendships with children of his own age. Both parents worked quite late and it was usual for David to come home from school on his own, let himself in, make his own supper and settle down to computer games. He had developed a ritual of cooking himself a large plate of french fries (which he knew were disapproved of because he was very overweight to the point of being obese), sitting down at the computer and munching away while playing extremely violent games. Though outwardly complacent and at ease with life, it is hard to think that this exterior was the whole story. In David's case, the computer games at which he would spend hours nightly were a necessary part of a ritual of anger and disobedience where forbidden foods and hidden violence were combined in the lonely hours after school.

CHAPTER SIX

SEXUAL DEVELOPMENT

At their own pace

The earlier chapters have described how ten year-old children differ very much from each other in their attempts to deal with increasing awareness of differences in ability and performance, as well as coping with group memberships and friendships. Up to now these issues have been looked at from a ten year-old perspective generally, rather than from a boy or girl perspective. It seems, however, that as far as developing sexuality is concerned the experience of boys and girls is different, though there are issues that are common to both.

Jokes and giggles

Same-sex groups provide a base within which some reinforcing of attitudes will take place. Like many other taboo subjects, boys and girls approach sexual matters usually through banter and giggles within their separate groups, but also through more direct poking fun at each other. "Knowledgeable" jokes by boys about sexual matters are quite common and perhaps are meant to convey to each other that there is a common fund of knowledge that boys have that means they don't have to worry about girls. For girls the issues will be different ones since some girls will have started periods and be more advanced physically than other girls, and than boys as a group. Having the giggles is one way to cope with anxieties and the tension of anxiety released within a little grouping of girls only. But as has been suggested earlier, a price needs to be paid for raising topics in this kind of setting. While providing a space for exploring some aspects of what it means to be a boy, or a girl, some of the groupings at this age can be very intolerant of differences and, in particular, of individuals who don't fit in to the group.

For example, Tony was a thoughtful, withdrawn boy who excelled in some areas of work at school but tended to keep himself on the outside of "gangs," even though he joined in and was good at some team activities. He struck up a very strong friendship with Frances, a petite girl who was also shy like himself. They would often go home from school together as friends, perhaps like a brother and sister who enjoyed each other's company. The two families knew each other and were pleased that such a bond, based on real affection, should be taking place, though they did joke a bit about Frances and Tony spending so much time together.

Both children found it difficult to be within close groupings of their own sex and it seemed they were both quite taken aback to find that their friendship gave rise to hostility within the class group as a whole. It was as if they had ventured, without realizing the issues involved, into areas which the strict rules of the groups wouldn't allow. Their friendship was made into something different by the class. Rude pictures were drawn and passed around as if the two children attracted from the group quite savage attacks on sexuality, particularly of a sexual couple. The group knew that these two were doing something unusual and had to make it "safe" by turning it into a relationship which was a parody of an adult sexual relationship.

The preoccupations of individual boys: transformers

It might seem strange to speak about sexuality in ten year-old boys. At first sight, it is an age which is relatively free from preoccupations about sexuality. On the whole, ten year-olds aren't yet having to cope with the bodily changes that mark progression into adolescence proper; boys in particular seem to be less well developed than girls of a similar age. It would be a mistake, however, to think that the group picture given above, with its emphasis on knowledgeable remarks and knowledgeable jokes, is the whole picture. Although ten can seem to be a time of consolidation, of a sense of knowing what one has achieved, it can also be a time where some very important changes are being played out in advance. The preoccupations of individual boys can seem far removed from sexuality, but when one looks more closely, one can see how connected they are with the bodily and particularly the emotional changes that will be taking place in the next few years.

Philip is typical of many boys of his age. He is fascinated by his collection of alien figures. Philip will be happily occupied for long periods of time acting out some inner play which seems to be much more fascinating than the stereotyped movements with which the figures themselves are pushed across the table. A typical figure is that of the gray plastic, armor-plated alien. Its face is covered with a visor and its legs, body and arms with armor. It is made up of parts which can be transformed to make an impregnable, formidable fighting machine armed with lethal weapons. Other figures within these collections are made out of soft, pliable rubber and can be stretched and pulled into different shapes. The game usually involves a lot of attack and counter-attack, destruction and the ability to regenerate after having been killed. Philip shows a seemingly endless enthusiasm for this continual warfare. Though the individual figures may vary, and the games themselves might be played out on a computer rather than with actual figures that can be held in the hand, the kinds of scenes that I have described will be familiar to many parents.

What to make of it all? There seem to be one or two common themes. The first is a fascination with the process of transforming in itself, the sudden changing from one state to another. The second is an interest in the nature of this transformation with different choices being selected, that of death or non-existence, of invulnerability, of flexibility and pliability. One way of thinking about all of this is to see these games as directly connected with the fascination in boys with the penis which in coming years will take on different properties. But what will these changes in the performance and size and shape of the penis mean? As well as being concerned with the penis itself, another way of thinking about these typical ten year-old games is that they are attempts to deal with anxieties. These anxieties attach themselves to the whole person; objects that get stretched are potentially felt to become weaker, more vulnerable. What is this change in sexuality that is on the horizon? What will it entail? Would it be better to deal with it by jumping into a monster skin, one which is impervious to attack? It is unlikely that anxieties such as these can be put into words, but the sheer enthusiasm of the ten year-old for games such as this suggest that they are much more preoccupied with the changes which are only on the horizon than they would be able to say.

. . . And of Individual Girls: looking ahead to periods

Girls of this age will, like boys, undoubtedly be aware of the bodily changes puberty will bring and will be thinking about it, or putting considerable energy into keeping it out of their minds. For most girls of this age the beginnings of puberty will still be on the horizon but some anxiety about bodily changes will be present, though likely hidden from themselves as well as from their parents. Ten year-old girls probably will have been told about the facts of life and about menstrual periods in particular. However it doesn't always follow that information leads to an increase in understanding.

Tracey had, it seemed, always misheard the word "womb" as "wound." There was nothing to let her know she had got it wrong; in fact many other ideas fitted together around this misconception so well that when it came out with three other girls giggling together in the playground about babies, she was very convincing to them about it. They half-believed her. After all, if it was a wound it would be expected to bleed. They had heard it hurt. It made sense.

The worry for Tracey would then be, what had happened to cause this damage inside? Was it something she had done to herself? Had she already done it? Was she just waiting for the damage to show? And when the wound did begin to bleed would her guilty secret that she had harmed herself, presumably through her masturbation, be found out?

These kinds of anxieties, like those of the boys, are very unlikely to be put into words, but Tracey's three friends, a bit upset by suddenly finding they didn't know what to believe, did turn to an adult to settle the question. It was important for them that they had someone to turn to whom they could trust not to laugh at them, but who would take their question seriously and explain things honestly.

Not many girls of ten will be having periods, so for those who do start ahead of the group as a whole the experience can be quite different than for those who start later. The sense of stepping away from their group of friends may then be stronger at this age than the feeling of pride in joining the wider group of womanhood; a ten year-old may not feel prepared for this, however ready her body might be.

Even for a girl who is well prepared as far as information goes, the first actual experience of her period can take her unawares. Trying to find in her mind the nearest thing to it that has happened before can then seem like a shameful loss of control, like wetting, or messing herself, as if she had suddenly gone backwards, not forwards in development. Asha in this situation, when her mother offered her sanitary protection, turned angrily on her saying that "she wasn't a baby. She wasn't going to wear diapers!"

When to call in help

There is an increasing awareness that a number of children, both boys and girls, may by the age of ten already have become the victim of child sexual abuse. Similarly, some may have grown up in circumstances which do not give them the opportunities over the years to develop their own sense of who they are, but instead subject them to perverse views and practices. The experience of being sexually assaulted or becoming involved in sexual activity with an adult leaves a marked effect on children. Some will let it be known if something like this has happened, but other children may find it much more difficult to speak openly about such traumatic things and may try to deny it to themselves. It can happen that an incident such as sexual assault can take place without any outward effect at the time, but then later, disturbing changes in behavior can take place. These are matters that need to be discussed with professional bodies such as child protection teams or child and family consultation centers.

CHAPTER SEVEN

HOLDING VIEWS

Rebellion at home

In this book, I have tried to put across the view that from the perspective of a ten year-old, "double figures" can be seen as confirming a process of growth, reaching the top of the pile, but also the start of something unknown. I would like to look in this chapter at some of the issues which will be introducing the ten year-old to a wider world than was previously the case. One of the most important developments is increasing concern about issues of justice and fairness. Much younger children can become very concerned when they feel that they themselves have been treated unfairly, but at ten, issues are seen as belonging to a wider stage than previously. It is quite likely that life at home is being made more uncomfortable. You may well find that views of your own which are held dearly are beginning to be challenged, not simply in an openly defiant way, but in a reasoned way. This may not be the sophisticated and passionate independence of the teenager, but the way in which a ten year-old can start to question authority can be every bit as disturbing.

David was a quiet child who could be rebellious and stubborn at home, but on the whole lived in the shadow of his father, who could be more intimidating than he intended. Almost overnight, David started to introduce alternative ideas. While not being openly defiant, he started to tell the family about a teacher whom he referred to as "Sir." Where the family ate meat, "Sir" talked about vegetarianism. Where the family used to go to church regularly, "Sir" had other ideas: many people didn't go to church and yet could be good people.

Within a relatively short space of time, "Sir" expressed strong views on almost every aspect of family life. At first, David's parents became worried. They began to wonder if he had fallen under the influence of "Sir." A meeting with "Sir" about routine school matters suggested to them that the "Sir" David brought home was far removed from the careful and professional teacher before them. They realized that "Sir" was a way hit upon by David of introducing ideas into the household which allowed him to think and to challenge the accepted way of doing things. It was as if he felt that because of the way things were done at home, he couldn't do this directly but had to import an authority in his mind who would be given credibility by the family, and who would be powerful enough to introduce new ideas.

The example illustrates how even to ten year-olds rules of the household can be revered because of their weight of tradition and authority in a way that parents may not realize. The fact that David, normally quite shy and retiring, should persevere with his systematic review of family values gives some idea of the strength of this push to broaden horizons:

- If it is church that makes people good, how are people good without church?
- Is it necessary to eat meat?
- Shouldn't we stop buying newspapers to save trees?

Although questions like this have been asked by your child before, there is a growing appreciation at ten that such questions are more complex than they seem at first. The process of deciding what one believes in, and the ability to free these beliefs from what has simply been accepted on authority, is a very important one. Equally crucial is that developing views like this should find a place within the family rather than have to be asked outside it.

The challenge to single parents

Sometimes the ideas being reviewed will involve not simply issues of practice, but affect the very constitution of the family itself. Mary had brought up her child single-handed. She hadn't intended it to be that way, but there had been a separation soon after Sarah was born. Sarah had become very bitter towards her father and for a few years had seemed to accept the fact that contact was not possible. She appeared to go along with Mary's view that seeing her father occasionally was more harmful than not seeing her father at all. At ten, she changed. Now she wanted to see him again. Mary, knowing that Sarah's father had many years ago put the relationship with her behind him and was now with someone else, felt that to make contact after all these years would be too painful for her, as well as for Sarah, and so she refused.

Although Sarah was cross and upset at first, she came to accept the decision and seemed to forget all about it. One day however, she wasn't in the usual place after school and Mary finally discovered that she had gone on a journey to try to find her father. Sarah had searched for Father's address and had made preparation for the journey, including taking her own as well as some of Mary's money.

The difficulties between Sarah and Mary are typical of the kinds of situations that can take place within families where there has been a break-up. There comes a point where decisions made by adults become public again, open to the gaze of ten year-olds. Sarah suddenly seemed to realize, in a more complex way than before, that Mary's decision not to keep up contact had implications for her as well. It can be very painful for adults to open up old wounds in this way. Decisions that had to be made have been made and all of a sudden they are coming under the gaze of ten year-olds. It can be very difficult at such times to keep private those matters which are not the business of ten year-olds, and at the same time to address the issue of how children do have rights in these matters.

It would be too easy to pretend that there is a simple answer to some of these questions. What should a family do if strong views are expressed which seem to be contrary to the major principles of living which are held by the family? How could a ten year-old understand the reasons which lay behind the need for separation and divorce? The main issue seems to be that ten year-olds are much more willing to bring into the household their own view and are becoming very competent at defending and justifying their viewpoint. It is important that the home is the place where they can be aired. By this I don't mean that what a ten year-old says should automatically change family policy, but it is important that the home should be the place where the development of one's own views should be heard rather than resisted. An important shift in the base of authority is taking place. Ten year-olds are not necessarily able to justify a point of view or stance with reasoned argument but, undoubtedly, are able to make their view heard with increasing firmness.

World issues

Arguing about rules in the family can be a preparation for arguing about, and having views about, the rules of the world community. It is highly likely that injustices in this arena will start to grate every bit as much as perceived injustices within the family. At times it may seem that world issues, with all their complexity, are approached with a simple model in mind, with very little patience for subtle shades of opinion. It may seem that action for starving children, environmental issues, vegetarianism, views about pets and many other issues are clung to with a conviction that has more to do with needing to express a view about the wider scene than establishing a priority among issues. It is important that space be given for ten year-olds to discover some of the rules (or lack of them!) which apply to bigger issues in the world.

Benjamin lived in a large house, one which had enough space to allow for undisturbed areas where activities could take place in peace. Pauline, his mother, was able to put up with invasions of the house, and was used to keeping a distant eye to make sure things did not get out of hand. One day Benjamin, normally a quiet child, came home having been completely captivated by a cause. He wanted to raise money for the victims of a natural disaster. He had invited some friends over and together they would work out the rules for their society which would then be able to raise money for charity.

It seemed to be an ambitious plan and Pauline made discreet inquiries as to whether her own services would be required in setting up this Society. She was firmly put in her place. This would be set up by children.

At first the small group of six were very enthusiastic and set about their task with eagerness. Soon, however, the sounds of argument filtered through the floorboards, and they were to become more intense as the new society began to run into trouble. The stumbling block was who would be the chairman. It seemed that this was a central issue and until it was settled no fundraising was likely. It became apparent to Pauline that in fact there was a great deal of fascination with the constitution-making process in itself. It seemed to become the main activity. It became clear that some of the group, once they had been invited to join, had brought some very strong opinions with them. They weren't convinced about the need for a leader and proposed a Committee. This wasn't at all what Benjamin wanted, for his enterprise was being taken over.

Hearing this put Pauline in a dilemma. Should she intervene? She was very tempted to do so and yet she hesitated because Benjamin had so much wanted this to be his own project. Eventually she decided not to. Constitutional issues proved too difficult to overcome and the enterprise was called off. Later she was able to discuss with Benjamin about how it failed and it was possible over time to look upon it as a very worthwhile way of discovering, through experience, how difficult it is to launch new ventures. As a bonus, the stumbling block in the way of the scheme, that is whether it would be led by one person or by more democratic means, made it possible to look at the way lines of authority within the family had been strained recently. Benjamin had been difficult to live with and had been particularly difficult in his relationships with his father to whom he was very challenging.

Eventually it was possible to plan together for a more modest fundraising event which was a success.

CHAPTER EIGHT

MOVING ON

Towards the end of their tenth year most children are becoming aware that they will have to begin to cope with challenging events within the next few years. At the beginning of the year it might have felt as if they were standing on the top of a mountain that had taken ten years to climb. By the end of the year the view from the top may look rougher and more unpredictable. The classroom scene will start to point more and more towards tests and examinations. Dreams of the future will start to be looked at in a more down-to-earth way and, little by little, will take on the shape of "career possibilities." There will be greater responsibility therefore, and by the end of the year most children will have much more of a sense of being in charge of the future, of being increasingly able to see themselves as teenagers in the making. By the end of the year, ten year-olds will probably feel that overall they have emerged from being small. Some girls will start to experience menstruation for the first time, moving away from anxious huddles about what is involved, to first-hand experience. Boys too will be developing a much more open ability to question adults, and to have views about sexual matters even though for most, puberty will still be some way in the future.

The move towards increased sexual awareness is a major change that somehow ten year-olds need to be prepared for, at least in some way, during the course of the year. Being plunged too quickly into situations that will be too much for them can be overwhelming.

Clearly, as we have seen, ten year-olds will develop at their own best speed, and progress will depend on general maturity as well as whatever adverse circumstances they have had to meet on the way. Even so, granted that there will be individual differences, it does seem possible to think of some general principles that will help ten year-olds to be ready to grow towards adulthood.

A place for being small

It might seem strange to look upon the ten year-old as needing a place to be small. How can this help ten year-old children to grow? Wouldn't it just encourage them towards babyishness, tempt them not to respond to the enormous events already mentioned and to curl up instead? Perhaps the thought does seem at first sight to go against logic but the example of Alan, considered earlier, has something important to offer here. You will remember that he found it difficult to relate to the other children in the class. He was awkward with them and extremely quick to protect himself. He might have been saying, "If they think they are going to hurt me then they are mistaken. " Instead of a frightened boy they will meet a well-armed warrior. For a boy like Alan, it would seem folly to think that he might cope better by being able to let himself feel small rather than defending against it. It might seem that he was being asked to agree to be annihilated.

Is it fair for a ten year-old to feel that he can face these enemies on his own? Doesn't a ten year-old child need a parent who will protect? There is no doubt about it. Parents should be able to provide protection when needed; to allow times for not being able to cope; for having a cuddle; even to going back to earlier habits for a time. Nobody will doubt that this will provide a safe place to retire to occasionally. But closely connected with the need for tolerant parents is the ability to tolerate one's own sense of being small and not being able to cope. After all, how can a ten year-old be confident of being able to cope with some of the main challenges to growth that are coming nearer? Is the best way to pretend that there is no problem, or to be able to appreciate that adult help is needed? It can be very reassuring to know that it is all right not to be able to cope.

Making friends

Some examples have already been given of how complicated a thing friendship is. Yvonne and Erin, you will remember, were in a mother and daughter relationship that was very intense following the breaking of Yvonne's relationship. When a new partner for Yvonne appeared, Erin was helped to cope with her feelings about the new relationship by finding a friend of her own age. Little by little she was able to pay less attention to Yvonne's adult relationship as she became more involved with her close friend. Certainly at first, Yvonne felt that Erin became less interested in her and she felt hurt by this. But the friendship, with its emphasis on activity, did make it possible for the relationship between them to become less intense, and for Erin to move away emotionally.

One important need that friendship fulfills is that it makes it possible for children to begin to try being more independent. At first this may involve spending more time out of the house, or in a part of the house that is not meant for adults! It may involve journeys away from home to relatives or with the school or other group to camp. It is the important beginnings of the process of leaving home at a much later age.

The need for involved parents

For parents, to know how much to let go at this stage of development is particularly difficult, in view of what was said earlier about accepting the need of ten year-old children to feel small as well as brave. This can be very hard to do when it is seen that your child is being caught up in a group situation, such as the classroom situation described earlier, or being in bad company. Knowing when to intervene or not can be difficult. However children who are isolated or very lost in groups are at a disadvantage. Difficult though it is, it is only in the rough and tumble of friendship and school that values can be tested, that loyalties can be forged and that children can begin to sort out what they believe in or not. They begin developing standards for themselves and others. That these are sometimes too rigid, sometimes too slack and other times just about right, can only be found out by experience. The move towards adulthood through the path of adolescence is one which doesn't have any precise starting point, but friendships start to have a different quality as junior high school age comes near. Although parental vigilance is necessary to prevent friendships going badly wrong, this is a healthier situation than isolation at this age. Some children, without being aware of it directly, might feel that they can jump into adulthood straight from ten, and miss out the problematic experience of puberty and adolescence.

Facing reality

Anita gave a very interesting view of the reality of being ten. She said that sometimes her mom was too strict, such as when she made her come in quite early after school instead of letting her play with her friends. This made her cross because she was old enough to look after herself now and decide how to run her life. Almost in the same breath she went on to say that there were times when she wished her mom wasn't so busy and could spend more time with her, and cuddle her like she used to do in the old days.

There was nothing to suggest that Anita's mother was particularly strict or that she didn't appreciate Anita's need for cuddles. But Anita obviously was feeling what being ten is about: caught somewhere between feeling very grown up and a much different state of feeling small. Inevitably being at the top of one mountain means that you can see bigger mountains to climb, if only you can persuade yourself to move away from your vantage point and grapple with the climb.

FURTHER READING

Children: Rights and Childhood, David Archard, Routledge 1993

Making Sense: The Child's Construction of the World, Jerome Bruner and Helen Haste Eds., Routledge 1990

Narratives of Love and Loss, Studies in Modern Children's Fiction, Margaret and Michael Rustin, Verso, London 1987.

The People in the Playground, Peter and Iona Opie, Oxford University Press 1993

THE AUTHOR

Jonathan Bradley is a Consultant Child Psychotherapist and Senior Tutor at the Tavistock Clinic. Before training as a Psychotherapist, he studied Psychology at Keele University and this was followed by research into how ten-eleven year-olds begin to develop sophisticated ways of thinking and reasoning. He has been a teacher and involved in a practical way with the running and development of clubs and organizations for young children. In addition to working at the Tavistock Clinic, he is a Child Psychotherapist within the Borough of Hackney where he works with teachers, schools and individual children and their parents. Jonathan Bradley is married with two children.

UNDERSTANDING YOUR CHILD
TITLES IN THIS SERIES

UNDERSTANDING YOUR BABY	by Lisa Miller
UNDERSTANDING YOUR 1 YEAR-OLD	by Deborah Steiner
UNDERSTANDING YOUR 2 YEAR-OLD	by Susan Reid
UNDERSTANDING YOUR 3 YEAR-OLD	by Judith Trowell
UNDERSTANDING YOUR 4 YEAR-OLD	by Lisa Miller
UNDERSTANDING YOUR 5 YEAR-OLD	by Lesley Holditch
UNDERSTANDING YOUR 6 YEAR-OLD	by Deborah Steiner
UNDERSTANDING YOUR 7 YEAR-OLD	by Elsie Osborne
UNDERSTANDING YOUR 8 YEAR-OLD	by Lisa Miller
UNDERSTANDING YOUR 9 YEAR-OLD	by Dora Lush
UNDERSTANDING YOUR 10 YEAR-OLD	by Jonathan Bradley
UNDERSTANDING YOUR 11 YEAR-OLD	by Eileen Orford
UNDERSTANDING YOUR 12-14 YEAR-OLDS	by Margot Waddell
UNDERSTANDING YOUR 15-17 YEAR-OLDS	by Jonathan Bradley & Hélène Dubinsky
UNDERSTANDING YOUR 18-20 YEAR-OLDS	by Gianna Williams
UNDERSTANDING YOUR HANDICAPPED CHILD	by Valerie Sinason

Price per volume: $8.95 + $2.00 for shipping and handling

Please send your name, address and total amount to:

WARWICK PUBLISHING INC.
388 KING STREET WEST • SUITE 111
TORONTO, ONTARIO M5V 1K2